King Commemorations:

A Collection of Activities, Volume 1

First Printing: March 2009

ISBN-10 1441463755

EAN-13 9781441463753
3 9082 11320 2801

FOREWORD
by
R. Cheryl Jones

Learning can be an awesome outlet for children, especially when fun and creativity are involved. This book contains both of those.

This composition of activities commemorates the life of one of the most admired men of our time, Martin Luther King, Jr.

Children, parents, and teachers alike, will enjoy the original, interesting, and fun activities that are presented.

Songs, skits, narrations, and poems are just a few of the ways we can learn about the life of Dr. King. This book gives a close-up view of his early life and childhood. It, also, gives ideas and suggestions to help children realize that one person can make a difference. But more than anything, it helps children to understand why it is so important to stand up for their beliefs.

PREFACE

Every third Monday in January, America commemorates the birthday of Dr. Martin Luther King, Jr.   He is the only African American who is honored by a National Holiday. His actual birthday is January 15, 1929. With the passing of time, many people, especially our children, are unaware of the significance of this Holiday. Why is it celebrated each year? What was so important about his accomplishments and life that our American Congress and President signed into law a Holiday honoring him?

Nearly every country has experienced some form of religious, racial, or social discrimination. America is no different. The history of slavery and associated cruelty in America made hypocrisy of its laws. History witnessed a nation representative of human rights strip some of its people of such rights. It was Dr. King's commitment to nonviolence, despite the opposition faced, that mobilized decent Americans to protest against the discriminatory Jim Crow Laws. The intent of this book is not to focus on what was, but to remember the past to prevent its reoccurrence. Also to imprint on the hearts of current and future generations, what one person can do when standing for the cause of justice.

In this generation, we can see the fruit of Dr. King's push for justice in the recent election of Barack Obama to the Presidency of the United States of America.   We have come a long way in one generation. It appears Americans thought more about the character of Obama than his color. This was the burning desire and dream of an African American in the mid-fifties and sixties. Forty years after his death, we see Dr. King's dream in action.

Often, school/community groups have programs or other activities with regard to this Holiday. Having spent many years writing materials for such celebrations in schools, Mrs. Elliott has compiled some of her writings to help others join the commemoration. Parents, educators and others should find this book useful as our youth are encouraged to be proactive about the welfare of others. *King Commemorations: A Collection of Activities, Volume 1 focuses* mainly on King's young life. It was obvious, even then, how events prepared and influenced him to become a great man.

TABLE OF CONTENTS

Section 3: Dramatizations 63

References 93

Section 1:

Songs

The songs in this section were written to be accompanied by common tunes, familiar to many such as, *"Twinkle, Twinkle Little Star."* If you do not know a tune, you may search the internet for a musical score or listen to its tune. The tunes may prove helpful while learning these songs. Also, italicized words/syllables signify these are to be sung as a joined note or intonation.

Often, commemorations are done during programs/assemblies. One of the best ways to commemorate Dr. King is through songs. Children enjoy singing and will readily learn the words. It is always helpful to make sure children understand what the words mean <u>before</u> singing/learning them. With the exception of one song, *"We Are Special,"* this section includes songs which have lyrics written to well-known tunes.

There are many ways to feature these songs as a part of your celebration, such as:

> ➤ If a song is used during a program, the audience may participate when the lyrics are printed on the program.

> ➤ Sometimes an entire grade/class may learn a verse to sing to the audience and the audience sings the chorus.

> Talented students may also be spotlighted with the verses.

> A choir may perform the verses or segment(s) while the audience participates by singing the chorus.

These suggestions are not intended to limit the use of these songs, but to springboard you into actions that best suit your circumstances.

Songs may be used in whole or in part. You may choose to have speaking parts from some of the narrative exercises between verses/choruses. You may use a song as your theme and have it interspersed throughout your celebration.

Whatever the case may be, these songs should be used for enjoyment while inspiring deeper life commitments to justice, teaching nonviolent principles, promoting peaceful actions to achieve justice, and focusing on the lessons learned from the life of Dr. King.

He Became Martin Luther
(Sung to the tune of "He's Got the Whole World in His Hands")

A child was born *in-in* Atlanta;
A January *day-ay*, the fifteenth,
In the year *nineteen-een* twenty-nine.
A sweet little boy named Michael.

He had a *sister-er* named Christine.
One day his *brother-er* A. D. came.
They lived in a *hou-ouse*, white and gray
With grandmother and grandfather.

Michael went to *school-ool* at age five
His teacher thought *he-e* was age six.
He told of his *cake-ake's* five candles;
So he was sent home for a year.

He loved to read *boo-ooks* and study
About people *in-in* history
Like the man with *his-is* father's name
Martin Luther was the name he liked.

Then Michael *Lewis-is* changed his name
So he would be *like-ike* his father
And that great man *he-e'd* read about;
Martin Luther was his new name.

SUGGESTED PROCEDURES: This is a fun song to include clapping while singing. Try using different handclaps – on beat, off beat, double time, etc. Foot stomping can be fun, too. Try different/alternating handclaps/foot stomping for each verse. You may even have one group sing while another does the rhythmic clapping and/or stomping.

Doing Wrong Won't Make Things Right
(Sung to the tune of "He's Got the Whole World in His Hands")

The King *family-ly* went to church
The kids were taught *to-o* do what's right,
To learn Bible ver-ses to recite,
And to help those who were in need.

Martin hated *when-en* kids were teased.
The bullies made *som-ome* children cry.
He had to stand *up-up* for their rights
Even when he got in trouble.

One day A. D. *was-as* teasing Chris.
Martin could not *get-et* him to stop.
He hit A. D.'s *head-ead* with the phone!
He was sad and promised to change.

He had to figure *ou-out* how to help
And not hurt the *one-one* doing wrong.
Martin knew two *wrong-ongs* couldn't make right
Any problem he had to fix.

Martin Luther *King-ing* would not fight.
He talked things out *to-o* make them right.
He solved problems *when-en* he got kids
To be kind to each other.

The Golden Rule *says-ays* treat others
Only in the *way-ay* that is right.
By being kind *and-and* fair to them
Just like you want to be treated.

SUGGESTED PROCEDURES: (See previous page.)

Once a Man
(Sung to the tune of "This Old Man")

Once a man, Dr. King,
Wanted peace that laws should bring.
Equal rights ought to come from
The laws of our land.
Freedom for all was his stand.

The marches that he led
To protest laws that were bad.
But some people said that these
Protests were a crime.
King was jailed time after time.

King told us, "No one's free
Till laws give all liberty."
Good laws protect all citizens
And not just a few.
Unless fair, laws just won't do!

Once a bomb hit King's house.
He told people not to fight.
Hatred is never really right.
Love must always be your rule
No matter what others do.

Laws were changed in our land
With King's pledge of nonviolence.
Often facing danger, King
Held to his belief
To fight wrongs with love and peace.

I will do all I can
To bring peace throughout our land.
Never to hate is my pledge,
But let my love show
So peace in this world will grow.

Will you do all you can
To bring peace throughout our land?
Never hating, will you pledge
And let your love show
So peace in our world will grow?

Dr. King

(Sung to the tune of "Twinkle, Twinkle, Little Star")

I have heard of Dr. King -
How he tried like everything
So people would live in peace
With no help from the police.
Listen to these words I sing -
Give your love, it's the best thing!

M. L. King didn't really like
When the bullies tried to fight.
They teased kids by making fun
So they cried and had to run.
Martin often made them quit
Not with muscles, but his wit!

M. L. King was very sad
Seeing what some people had.
Some didn't have enough to eat
Or some shoes upon their feet.
The Kings felt it was their call
To share and not keep their all.

His dad taught him as a child
To help others so they smiled.
They gave clothes to those in rags
And put food into some bags.
They made many people glad
'Cause they shared those things they had.

I am glad for what King did
Starting when he was a kid.
He sought justice for us all
Using his nonviolent call.
We should follow him today -
Helping in a peaceful way.

The Cause of Justice
(Sung to the tune of "Climb Ev'ry Mountain")

("Climb Ev'ry Mountain" has four verse-like parts. This song has **five**. Just remember the first three parts are identical in tune to the original song. The last two parts of this song are exactly like the last two parts in *"Climb Ev'ry Mountain."*)

Great is the diff'rence
When you do right
For the cause of justice
You should stand and fight.

Some people wanted
To right the wrong
By fighting with more force
Without love along.

But Dr. *King-ing*
Taught people how
To change those unfair laws
For the justice cause.

The dream King had of
Freedoms for you and me
Burned deep within his heart
'Cause all men should be free

Stand up for justice
And do what's right.
In peace and in love take
Up the justice fight!

King's Destiny of Love

(Sung to the tune of the "Impossible Dream.")

It was the destiny of King
That he would hear his noble call.
So King stood in peaceful resistance
To start an injustice downfall.

King fought against a mighty source.
He used the best peaceful recourse,
Though he faced all types of evil force.
Still King vowed a nonviolent course!

It was King's pledge to always do right,
Regardless how hateful some others did fight.
King did not waver, but took courage in flight
And he stood as a peaceful warrior in his predestined
        plight!

King taught us to stand up for the just
With God's love in each heart.
So we will always be the winners
Right from the very start.

And our land is much better because
King showed us how to reach high above
And to conquer hatred with our love.
King's destiny was reached with love.

SUGGESTED PROCEDURES: This is a great song for a solo
or duet. A choir may even sing various parts with the solo/duet.
This song should be moving with intense feelings and leading
to a climax at the end.

Dr. King, Amen!
(Sung to the tune of the Negro Spiritual, "Amen")

Notations
(L) – Lead Soloist(s)   (C) – Choir, rest of group, or Audience

Prelude
(C) A-a-a-a-men! A-a-a-a-men! *A - a –* men!
A – men! A – men!"

Verse 1
(L)	Once there was a *boy-oy*.	**(C)**	A-a-a-a-men!
(L)	Whose name was Michael Lewis.	**(C)**	A-a-a-a-men!
(L)	Born in *Atlan-anta*.	**(C)**	*A - a –* men!
			A – men! A – men!

Verse 2
(L)	He had a big sister.	**(C)**	A-a-a-a-men!
(L)	Then his brother *cam-ame -*	**(C)**	A-a-a-a-men!
(L)	A really close threesome.	**(C)**	*A - a –* men!
			A – men! A – men!

Verse 3
(L)	Like so many children,	**(C)**	A-a-a-a-men!
(L)	They looked for tricks to *play-ay*.	**(C)**	A-a-a-a-men!
(L)	So they got in trouble.	**(C)**	*A - a –* men!
			A – men! A – men!

Verse 4
(L)	The kids had lots of *fun-un*,	**(C)**	A-a-a-a-men!
(L)	Playing with their *frien-ends*.	**(C)**	A-a-a-a-men!
(L)	In their big, *backyar-ard*.	**(C)**	*A - a –* men!
			A – men! A – men!

Verse 5
(L)	His folks said it was *fin-ine*	**(C)**	A-a-a-a-men!
(L)	For him to change his *na-ame;*	**(C)**	A-a-a-a-men!
(L)	He became Martin Luther.	**(C)**	*A - a –* men!
			A – men! A – men!

Verse 6

(L)   Their father was preacher;   (C)   A-a-a-a-men!
(L)   Their mom was a teacher,   (C)   A-a-a-a-men!
(L)   The Kings had a good life.   (C)   *A - a –* men!
                                          A – men! A – men!

Verse 7

(L)   They knew what was *righ-ight*.   (C)   A-a-a-a-men!
(L)   Their parents taught them *well-ell* (C)   A-a-a-a-men!
(L)   And showed them how to *liv-ive..* (C)   *A - a –* men!
                                          A – men! A – men!

Verse 8

(L)   Still, the Kings helped others,   (C)   A-a-a-a-men!
(L)   Whom they saw in *nee-eed.* (C) A-a-a-a-men!
(L)   Always lending a hand.   (C)   *A - a –* men!
                                          A – men! A – men!

Finale

(C)   A-a-a-a-men! A-a-a-a-men! *A - a –* men!
        A – men! A – men!"

SUGGESTED PROCEDURES: Sing verses (Lead Solos) with appropriate feelings. For example the seventh Lead should be sung very solemnly. For effectiveness, the "Amens" should vary in intensity and volume.

Let Peace and Love Live On
(Sung to the tune of "Battle Hymn of the Republic")

Verse 1
Some time ago, there lived a man named Martin Luther King.
He dreamed of peace for everyone that only love could bring.
He knew nonviolence was the way to bring about a change.
A change in unfair laws.

Chorus   (Remember to sing after each verse.)
"Glory, glory, Hallelujah. . . *(Repeat twice.)* . . ."
Let peace and love live on.

Verse 2
King knew that all God's people must respect man's dignity.
The young or old and Black or White in this society
Must have an equal justice, if our laws are to survive
And stand the test of time.   **Chorus**

Verse 3
King taught us how to protest and the meaning of sit-in.
He used these peaceful weapons for all troubles thick-and-thin.
He knew from God Almighty that de-li-ver-ance would come,
If we kept faith in Him.   **Chorus**

Verse 4
Though beat and jailed so *of-often*, he never thought to hate -
To hate would only bring more hate and make us small, not
        great.
But with our love we'll conquer evil hatred seen in men
And bring them to their knees.   **Chorus**

Verse 5

He won the Nobel Prize for Peace in 1964.
But all the money he received was given o the poor.
He knew they were the ones who faced discrimination most
And needed justice then.   **Chorus**

Verse 6

Now, since we all are kindred, we must try to live in peace,
Believing in Almighty God to make our love increase.
Forget the past of evil; to the world our love release
And God will then bless us.   **Chorus**

SUGGESTED PROCEDURE: This is an excellent song for
different groups, e.g. classes, grades or clubs, to learn a verse
to perform while everyone else sings the chorus after each
verse.

The Laws of our Land
(Sung to the tune of "This Land Is Your Land")

Some laws of this land
Were known as Jim Crow;
They made it so hard
For Blacks to live; so,
Along came a great man
Who just wanted justice -
His name was Martin Luther King!

King said, "We will not
Obey unjust laws.
We need the same rights
Given to all others,
For we're a family
Of sisters and brothers.:"
His name was Martin Luther King!

Protests were started;
Folks stood for justice.
They marched for freedom,
Using nonviolence.
Police tried to stop them
With their dogs and hoses.
They marched with Martin Luther King!

Are the laws good for
All of a nation,
If they don't protect
Each of its citizens?
Without this guarantee,
There is never justice
Protested Martin Luther King!

Once in our Country

(Sung to the tune of "This is my Country")

Once in this country
All were not free.
Laws in our country
Lacked decency.
Jim Crow divided us; yet,
America had ruled
The rights in our country
Are for everyone!

King said, "My country
Must keep her pledge.
We love our country.
Let's take a sledge
Of love and nonviolence -
Shatter unfair laws.
We'll stand for justice and
Disobey bad laws!"

Folks in our country
Marched on and on,
Wanting our country
To be as one.
Believing people should be
Given equal rights,
By laws in this country
For Blacks just like Whites.

Then in our country
Some got irate;
They felt our country
Was just first-rate.
Black people have liberty
They've rights and are free -
Separate but equal
Jim Crow guaranteed.

Cops in our country
Felt they must break
Folks in our country;
'Twas a mistake!
With force of dogs and water,
Police tried to stuff
Marches of a people
Who had had enough.

King made our country
Go on a hunt;
Peace in our country
Was the forefront.
King said, "Never hate, but love
'Cause we'll be free;
In our search for freedom,
We'll have dignity!"

So in our country
Changed laws were earned.
Folks in our country
A moral learned.
There is a price for justice
All of us must pay.
All or none can be free;
It's the only way!

This is your country
Let's hear your voice.
Speak in your country;
Make right your choice.
People should be respected
For whom they are
Not be judged by color,
But by character.

We are Special!
(Sung to the tune of the "Goodbye My Coney Island Baby")

Verse
I am special. You are special.
We can live like King.
King was a famous man
Who wanted peace for all.
He wanted freedom
For Blacks and Whites alike.
He wanted everyone
To have the *same-ame* rights!

Chorus 1
I'm a very special *per-erson*.
You're a very special person, too.
We hold a *dream-eam of-of jus-ustice*
And a world of sisterhood!

Chorus 2
I'm a very special *per-erson*.
You're a very special person, too.
We hold a *dream-eam of-of jus-ustice*
And a world of brotherhood!

See the next two pages for musical score.

We are Special!

We are Special! *(Cont')*

Fight Songs

The song, *We Are Special*, may be adapted as a fight song for a school or club.   I used this as a fight song for various schools by changing the first line of the verse and the first two lines of each chorus.

Examples of Changes:

Title: King Cobra
Verse: I'm a Cobra. You're a Cobra
Chorus: I am just a King Kid Cobra.
              You are just a King Kid Cobra, too.

Title: Forsythe Vikings
Verse: I'm a Viking. You're a Viking
Chorus: I am just a Forsythe *Vi-i-king*.
              You are just a Forsythe Viking, too.

Title: Abbot All-Stars
Verse: I'm an All-Star. You're an All-Star
Chorus: I am just an Abbot *All-All*-Star.
              You are just an Abbot All-Star, too.

SUGGESTED PROCEDURES: Remember, the other words remain the same. Have fun with this. Invite children to adapt this song for a school's/club's fight song so they feel a sense of ownership.

Cheers

Try doing some cheers **before** singing the fight song.

Leader	Audience
"Give me a K."	"K"
"Give me an I."	"I"
"Give me a N."	"N"
"Give me a G."	"G"
"What does it spell?"	"King" (soft)
"What?"	"King" (louder)
"I can't hear you!"	"King" (loud)
Everybody:	"Yeah-h-h-h-h-h!"

Other Word Cheers:

Love, Share, Peace, Unity, Justice, etc.

Ballad of Martin Luther King

(Sung to the tune of "The Ballad of Davy Crockett")

Born in Atlanta, he was very small.
That Tuesday morn, he hardly cried at all.
Now his older sis' with his mom and dad
Made four in the family, if you add.
Martin Luther *King-ing*: champion of civil rights!

His life began on a cold, dreary day.
'Twas January fifteenth, not in May.
It was the year 1929.
Depression was coming; the Kings were fine.
Martin Luther *King-ing*: champion of civil rights!

He was taught how to help his fellow man;
Seeing their need, he gave a helping hand,
The Kings got people at church to help out
So the poor didn't have to worry or doubt.
Martin Luther *King-ing*: champion of civil rights!

Black children were not allowed in the school
Where white children went; it was the rule.
They couldn't get together and even play;
By Jim Crow Laws, it was not okay!
Martin Luther *King-ing*: champion of civil rights!

He was good at school and learned very fast.
Helping others was part of his past;
So, it was no chore to do all he could
To help kids learn things the way they should.
Martin Luther *King-ing*: champion of civil rights!

When taunting bullies would come along
And they were much bigger and very strong,
King got them to give back things they didn't own
To the smaller kids and leave them alone!
Martin Luther *King-ing*: champion of civil rights!

Martin King saw despair in the faces
Of people going to many places.
He had to do something to stop their plight;
So, he stepped up and joined their fight.
Martin Luther *King-ing*: champion of civil rights!

He fought for the justice of everyone.
He never thought about using a gun.
He said, "Nonviolence is the only way."
So hundreds marched with him day after day.
Martin Luther *King-ing*: champion of civil rights!

One day he told us, *"I Have a Dream."*
Folks had had enough and it did seem
America would live up to its creed
With laws of justice everyone did need.
Martin Luther *King-ing*: champion of civil rights!

King took up folks' causes who were poor
For unfair treatment they had to endure.
The Nobel Prize for Peace in sixty-four
Gave King thousands to use for the poor.
Martin Luther *King-ing*: champion of civil rights!

"I've Been to the Mountaintop," and we've won.
In Tennessee his work here was done
In April 4, 1968 sun,
King was shot dead with a sniper gun!
Martin Luther *King-ing*: champion of civil rights!

Section 2:

Poems &
Narrative Expressions

These exercises are intended to teach about the early life of Dr. King. They should also provide enjoyment, inspiration and motivation. The ultimate goal, however, is a personal commitment to pursue justice through peaceful means.

This section contains exercises that you may modify for your situation. With just a little rehearsal time, individuals and groups of children (large and small) can participate. Continue to adapt them until you have included each child. Rehearsals are best when individuals have learned their parts. The use of an overhead or slide projector may be used when exercises are adapted for a monologue. The suggestions are a result of previous experiences in presenting these narrations.

King, the Child from A to Z

Provide visual progression of this exercise by using 26 large cards. Each card should have a different CAPITAL letter of the alphabet. Arrange children in an arc or line(s) making sure each is seen. Here are some ways to include ALL children:

1. Use enough extra cards to assure ALL have a part.
2. There are 28 speaking parts. You may decide to have 26-28 cardholders, too.
3. You may combine speaking parts for your situation.
4. The introductory speaker may also be the closing speaker.
5. Two children may share the introductory/closing part(s).
6. Children may recite parts for consecutive letters.
7. All children may have their drawings and parade afterwards showing them to the audience, as they sing at the end or just walk around. You may even call it the *"Cavalcade of King, the Child."*
8. The song, "He Became Martin Luther," on page 11 is excellent with this exercise.

When the title is said at the beginning, you may have children fan the letters of the alphabet. For example, when children say "A to Z," have the letters go up and down quickly from A to Z like a wave. Each letter may also be turned over to show the letters in a wave effect. Practice having the children pause for a few seconds to allow all the cards to be shown. You may want to have the cardholders in front so the letter fanning may be seen more easily. Then, they may move behind the speakers.

Most of all, remember that the options are endless. Be innovative!

King, the Child from A to Z

ALL: "King the Child from A *(Pause while the letters are fanned or moved in a wave fashion.)* to Z"

We've come to honor Dr. King,
A great American.
He sought to make laws fair for all
And was a peaceful man.
To tell about his childhood, we
Will go from A to Z.
Before he became famous, he
Started as just a baby.

A is for **Atlanta**, Georgia,
The town where he was born,
On January 15th
Early that Tuesday morn.

B is for their **big backyard** where
Lots of kids came to play.
A basketball court and much more
Made for a fun-filled day.

C is **careful crib care** given
The Kings' first boy so small.
Although named Michael Lewis, he
Was called M. L. by all.

D is for the **dashing deeds done**
By M. L. as a lad
He stood against taunting bullies
Who took what small kids had.

E is **eagerness** to learn.
At five, he went to school.
Miss Dickerson sent him home 'cause
He wasn't six by the rule.

F is the **firehouse** down the street
Where M. L. and friends went.
As they talked and checked the fire trucks,
Many fun hours were spent.

G is for **games** that M. L. played,
Using any size ball.
Smaller that A. D., his brother,
He always gave his all.

H is the **happy home** he knew.
The Kings had lots to share,
As they fed and gave others clothes;
For the Kings, this wasn't rare.

I is his **interests** so keen
In many things he had.
Getting another book to read
Always made M. L. glad!

J is his **jobs** - delivering
Paper, taking out trash
Or peeling some potatoes for
Grandma Jeannie to mash.

K is for the **kitchen** where the
Kings had a lot to do -
Like fixing meals and bagging food
More times than just a few.

L is for the **love** M. L. got
Each day from friends and kin.
He learned to respect everyone
With love that's genuine.

M is the **made-up** games he played
With two white friends each day.
When they started school, his friends' folks
Wouldn't let them come to play.

N is for the **napkin** his mom used
To dry away each tear.
"M. L., you're just as good as them!"
She said, making it clear.

O is for the **organ** his mom played
While M. L. sang solos.
Money earned for singing
Helped lessen poor folks' woes.

P is for **piano** lessons
Taught by Mr. McMann.
M. L. helped unscrew the stool's legs -
Teacher fell on his can!

Q is for each **quarter** M. L.
Earned for the work he did.
To work for your money is what
He learned when just a kid.

R is for the **races** M. L.
Ran with a lot of speed.
Often at the end of a race
M. L. was in the lead.

S is for **shoes** that he didn't get
Because the salesman said,
"YOU NEGROES, use those seats back there!"
They left those shoes instead!

T is the **telephone** M. L.
Used to hit A. D.'s head
Because he kept on teasing Chris.
M. L. was anger led!

U is for his **understanding**
Of what was right and wrong.
His dad's sermons and the Bible
Made his conscience quite strong!

V is for the **verses** learned and
He always knew his part.
At dinner, the King children said
Their Bible verses by heart.

W is the **wordy words** M. L.
Loved to hear and repeat.
The bigger the word used, the more
M. L. thought it was sweet!

X is the **x-ray** not taken
When hit by a big truck!
M. L. unhurt with his wrecked bike,
Was much more than just luck!

Y is the "**Yes**," he said each time
To always do his best.
His talents and lots of hard work
Won more than one contest.

Z is the **zest** M. L. had and
He loved to play this trick:
Scaring passing folks by shaking
Grandma's fur on a stick!

M. L. learned to love and respect
People despite their faults.
He helped change America by
Disobeying bad laws.
He was determined to right the
Wrongs without going wild.
Before Dr. King was famous,
He was only a child.

ALL: "King the Child from A. . ."
(Pause while letters are swung upward from left to right to chest
or top of head. Motions should be smooth and fast as a wave.)
ALL: ". . . to Z!"
(A person in the back facing the children should signal when to
say the last line, as they cannot see the wave.)

Have children bow/curtsy once or twice in unison afterward.

NOTE: This work will later be featured in a classic coloring
book.

Martin, the Kid

Martin King was once a kid
Just like you and me.
He played games and sometimes hid
Or the "IT" he'd be!

Martin had a sister, Chris,
And brother, A. D.
A chance for fun they didn't miss -
Such a lively three!

Martin, often tops at school,
Loved reading the best.
He tried to follow each rule
And pass every test.

Martin learned it was his duty
To help others out.
He'd stand up to the bully
Who pushed kids about.

Martin helped other kids see
Fractions weren't so bad.
He showed them just how easy
Fractions were to add.

Martin was small for his age.
He used words to win,
Instead of fists in a rage.
His words made heads spin!

Martin was once a small kid
Who tried to obey.
Mostly right was what he did
By the Bible's way.

M-A-R-T-I-N . . .Martin!

Middle child in the King family
Above average ability
Ready with words to convince you to agree
Trained to treat people with dignity
Ideas to try that were many
Never stop making others happy.

M-A-R-T-I-N . . .Martin!

SUGGESTED PROCEDURES:
1) Use 6 cards with CAPITAL letters for the name Martin.
2) All the children should say the first and last lines, which are identical.
3) Children spell his name, raising the lettered cards one by one in a smooth wave action.
4) After this wave action, children pause (two or three counts) and then say, "Martin."
5) Letters should then be lowered or placed out of sight.
6) As each child speaks, his/her corresponding letters should be raised during the child's line.
7) Once line is spoken, the letter may be lowered to chest or abdomen, but in view.
8) After all the lines are recited, children should repeat the opening by spelling Martin's name while fanning the letters.
9) During this last pause, letters should be raised to the highest position possible before saying the name, "Martin!"
10) Children should bow/curtsy once or twice in unison afterwards.

"The Young Michael Lewis King"

1. On January 15, 1929, a lot was happening at 501 Auburn Street in Atlanta, Georgia. Since a flu epidemic was rapidly spreading in the city, this two-story, 12-room house had been cleaned from top to bottom. Kettles of steaming water were in the kitchen. Several friends and neighbors came and went as they made sure everything was ready. Why?

2. A Black mother was having a baby. During the 1920's, Black mothers were not admitted to hospitals in the South. So this mother was made comfortable at home with a doctor in attendance. When this little baby was born, the doctor was not sure he was alive because he was so still and quiet. But with a quick WHACK on the bottom, the baby began to cry, softly.

3. This tiny newborn was the first son of the Rev. Michael Lewis King and Mrs. Alberta Christine King. They named the infant Michael Lewis King, Jr. Willie Christine, the Kings' older child, was excited by all the commotions. At a year and a half, she was a BIG sister. She had been born in September of 1927.

4. The Kings had married on Thanksgiving Day, November 25, 1926. They had lived with Mrs. King's parents, the Williamses – Rev. Adam Daniel Williams and Mrs. Jeannie Celeste Parks Williams. Rev. Williams was the renowned pastor of the Ebenezer Baptist Church located at the corner of Auburn Avenue and Jackson Street. Rev. King pastored two small churches: one in East Point and the Traveler's Rest Baptist Church. Preferring to be independent, Rev.

King refused several times to be an assistant pastor for Ebenezer.

5. On July 30, 1930, the Kings had their third child, Alfred Daniel. He was given Mrs. King's father's middle name. Now, Michael was a BIG brother when he was a year and a half. As Michael grew, his mother realized he was a very bright child. Mrs. King was a teacher and taught her children to read. The parents also taught the children to think before taking actions.

6. At four years old, Michael, or M. L. as he was called, sang beautiful soprano solos in churches and at church conventions. His mother played the organ. M. L. often sang, *"I Want to be (More) Like Jesus."* When the churches gave him a "love" offering, the money was used to help others. Since this was during the Great Depression, many people were in need. There were always lots of people to help.

7. In the spring of 1931, Rev. Williams was playing with 3-year-old Chris in the living room when he had a heart attack! Chris went into the kitchen to report that Grandpa fell asleep! A short time after the death of Rev. Williams, Rev. King became the pastor of the Ebenezer Baptist Church. Michael often heard his father encourage the church members to stand tall and be proud of themselves. He saw many poor families given food and clothes from the church and their home.

8. In 1933, Rev. King's father became ill. He begged Rev. King to make Martin Luther his official name because it was the one he had given him at birth. Rev. King's parents always disagreed on his name, but Mr. King insisted the two names of his brothers were Michael's name. Shortly after James

Albert King died, Rev. King became Rev. Martin Luther King with official papers.

9. The King kids were great friends and did nearly everything together. When Chris went to Younge Street School in the fall of 1934, M. L. insisted on going, too. He convinced his mother that she should let him go. The teacher, Miss Dickerson, enjoyed her new student, M. L. One day, M. L. was telling the kids about his birthday cake with FIVE candles on it. Then, Miss Dickerson knew he was not six years old and would have to leave school. Sadly, M. L. had to go home. Because the private university school had no room for a new student at that time, M. L. had to wait a year before going to school.   Mrs. King continued teaching him. When he returned to school, he was promoted to second grade, skipping first grade.

10. M. L. always played with his brother, Alfred, who was called A. D. The Kings had a big backyard that was like a small park, especially with the vacant lot next door. Rev. King and the boys even set up a spot for basketball. The King threesome and the neighborhood kids had plenty of room to play.

11. Across the street was a general store. The white storeowners had two boys about the same ages as the King boys. These four boys, and other kids in the neighborhood, were constant playmates. One day in August of 1935, the mother of the two white boys would not let them come out to play. When M. L. asked her, "Why?" She said angrily, "Because they can't play with you Negroes anymore!" M. L. was stunned! He went home in tears.

12. It was M. L.'s first time to really understand what it meant to be a Black child in the South. The Kings had protected their

children from the injustices around them by not using the buses, not going to the movie shows, not visiting Grant Park, and on and on.

13. Mother Dear tried to explain that it was the way things were done: Blacks and Whites were to live separately according to the Jim Crow Laws. Mrs. King also told her children that people just did not understand we are all the same, but one day things would be different. Through his tears, M. L. promised very sternly, "Mother Dear, one day I'm going to turn this world upside down."

14. M. L. did not like this segregation or separation of the races! By the laws, it was a crime for Blacks and Whites to use the same water fountains, go to the same school, use the same restrooms, use the same doors to buildings, ride the elevator at the same time, play checkers together and many, many more bizarre regulations. The laws said "separate, but equal." Looking around, anybody would know things were separate, but definitely not equal.

15. Rev. King did not like these laws either. One day, M. L. and his dad went to Five Points downtown to buy some shoes. They sat in seats at the front of the store. The salesman offered them seats in the back. Rev. King assured him their seats were just fine. When the salesman insisted that they sit in the old, raggedy seats in the back of the store, Rev. King stormed out of the store saying that he would not spend his money there. M. L.'s father would not buy him those shoes because he could not sit where he wanted.

16. Now, Michael loved to read and learn about people and the world. M. L. spent his allowance and the money he earned as a paperboy (the part he was allowed to spend) on books and more books. M. L. really enjoyed playing, too. He

skated, played marbles, flew kites, rode his bike, played a lot of ball, and even invented games.

17. The Kings wanted the best for their children. Once, Mrs. King decided that all her children would learn to play the piano. Mr. McMann was hired to teach them. Now, he was strict about playing correctly. When wrong notes were played, Mr. McMann would rap their knuckles with a ruler! One day the boys who wanted to play outside, not on the piano, unscrewed the legs on the stool before Mr. McMann came. When he sat down, the stool fell over and so did Mr. McMann! M. L. still learned to play a few songs, despite his lack of interest.

18. The King children had a lot of fun, even when they played pranks. They had a favorite prank. They would tie their grandmother's fox fur piece on a long stick. This fur piece had glassy eyes with a dark nose. Then, they would hide in the hedges in front of their home just before dark. When people passed by, they would push out the fur piece and shake it. You could hear screams up and down the street. What fun they had scaring people half to death!

19. The Kings were very firm with their three children about the really important things. There was no discussion about the time to do certain things: there was a time to work, a time to read or study and a time to play. The Kings also taught their children how to manage money. They had the **Three S-Rule** about money. One third of their money had to be **S**aved, one third **S**hared and the last third could be **S**pent.

20. M. L. read a great deal about Martin Luther. He was a religious leader who lived in the 15th century. He took a stand for what he believed was right, even though it went against their church's teachings. M. L. admired his father

who always stood up for what he believed was right, even in the face of danger or punishment. Since his Dad had changed his name, they had different names now.

21. Michael decided he wanted to change his name to Martin Luther. He first told his cousin, Willie Ponder. M. L. explained that if he changed his name, he would have the same name as his dad and the famous religious leader - two great men who were important to him. M. L.'s parents agreed to this change, and so today, we know him as Martin Luther King, Jr.

22. M. L. also had several scares in his young life. Playing on the stairs, he fell twenty feet down into the cellar landing on his head! Later, he was hit by a truck while riding his bike on a downtown street. The bike was a wreck! M. L. was bruised, but fine. Once as he played catcher in a baseball game, the bat flew out of A. D.'s hand and hit M. L. in the head! M. L. shook it off and said, "That was three strikes. You're out!" When Grandma Jeannie died, M. L. wanted to die, too! He jumped out his bedroom window! Because M. L. survived these scares and others, he grew up and helped America to be a better nation.

SUGGESTED PROCEDURES:

1. Use several speakers for these parts. You may even use 22 speakers, one for each part. You may choose 3 – 7 speakers who alternate parts.
2. Have children make posters to represent each speaking part.
3. Use soft background music or sound effects for each part. (A slide show is being developed for this exercise which will be available in the near future for purchase.)

"What Martin Learned About. . ."

"What Martin Learned about LOVE!"   *(SIGN)*

1. You must love God.
2. Love people like you love yourself.
3. You must love everybody, even your enemies.
4. Everybody needs love.

"What Martin Learned about GOD!"   *(SIGN)*

1. God is love.
2. We must love God and the people He created.
3. God made us all the same.

"What Martin Learned about SHARING!"   *(SIGN)*

1. Everybody needs someone else.
2. What you have is better when it is shared.
3. You must see and meet the needs of other people.
4. You have great joy when you share.

"What Martin Learned about Money!"   *(SIGN)*

1. You must earn money.
2. All money is a gift from God.
3. Use money to show thanks to God.
4. Use money to help others first, then yourself.
5. Always save some of your money.

"What Martin Learned about FAMILY!"   *(SIGN)*

1. Family supplies our needs for food, shelter and clothing.
2. Family provides love and protection.
3. We are all a part of the human family.
4. We must be concerned about the welfare of each other.
5. We are responsible for living together peacefully.

SUGGESTED PROCEDURES:

1. Have a child hold up a sign (hereafter called the sign holder) with the Word Title for that section, e.g. LOVE, MONEY, etc.
2. You may use as many of these parts as you choose from each group, as well as the order in which they are presented.
3. Sign holder announces his/her group by stepping forward and saying: "What Martin Learned about LOVE" for example.   You may also have **all** the children in each group say the title for that section.
4. Then, the sign holder moves a fair distance over and back.
5. One by one, children step forward telling the lesson Martin learned as a child.
6. As each child completes his/her speaking part, she/he should join the sign holder.

Play No More

There was a time when all seemed quite well.
A life of fun filled each day. 'Twas swell!
Out of the blue came a hurt so deep,
Arousing senses that were asleep.

Across the street he went like before.
He stepped inside the general store.
"Hi!" he said as friendly as can be
"Won't you come outside and play with me?"

Michael just wanted them to come play,
As they had done most everyday.
"We can't come to play," was the reply.
It was then M. L. asked the boys, "Why?"

From the tall counter, their mom stepped out.
With harsh words of anger she lashed out.
"You ain't nothing just a black Negro!
My boys ain't playing with you no mo'!"

Bewildered and hurt he left that place.
As he ran home tears ran down his face.
"Mother Dear!" was Michael's call so strong.
He was safe in her arms before long.

She held him and listened while he cried.
And with a hanky each tear she dried.
When he settled down, he heard her speak,
"God made you so special and unique!"

"M. L., you must learn what folks may feel
Is a far, far cry from what is real.
White folks think they are the better race
And us Black folks should stay in our place."

Michael said, "I don't see how that's true.
They are just people like me and you."
"You are right, but they don't understand,"
His mom said. "We're all one human brand."

"It'll be different one day, you'll see.
Never forget your are **somebody**!
You remember all I said is true;
God loves you so and I love you, too!"

Without tears and a determined stare
"I will do something," he did declare.
"One day I'll turn this world upside down!
We'll all be the same in every town!"

Try It Martin's Way

Why stand apart as strangers,
When we have so much to share?
We should not be "Lone Rangers"
And pretend we just don't care.
We need each other today,
As we never did before.
Let us try it Martin's way:
Joined in peace and love galore!

Let us take no time to hate
For injustices will fail.
Just walk a united gait,
With peaceful love we'll prevail!
Many things we can achieve
When together we all stand
Defending what we believe
As our rights that we demand.

We should strive to make things right.
Never forsaking the fight
That Martin fought yesterday.
But, let's try it Martin's way.

Remember!

Martin Luther King said
To love one another
Because everyone is
Our sister or brother.
The world will not have peace
Until love we release.
Society is not
A peaceful place just yet;
So show love to others-
This you must not forget!

You and Me
(Chant)

If peace is *(Clap, clap.)* ever to be *(Clap, clap.)*,
It is up to *(Clap, clap.)* you and me!   *(Say this slowly pointing appropriately to audience then self.)*

(Repeat three times saying louder each time.)

The Names King

As just a baby boy his given name
Was Michael Lewis. His dad's was the same.
For a shorter name, M. L. he became.
But, he was called Mike, Jr. now and then,

This little boy had counted names of three:
Michael, Mike, Jr., and M. L., you see.
This was the start of his names-a-plenty.
Although not intended, that's how it went.

The parents of Michael's dad didn't agree
On his name. They argued, "What will it be?
Michael Lewis or Martin Luther?" See,
They never agreed and just let it go!

After his mama was long gone, his dad
Reminded him about the name he had.
He said, "Before I die, please make me glad
And make Martin Luther your proper name."

"See, I named you Martin for my brother
And Luther is for my younger brother.
Promise me you'll take these and no other;
Then, I'll rest in peace wanting nothing more."

As he promised by Grandpa King's deathbed,
Mike's dad became Martin Luther instead.
This was how his official papers read.
That's how he became Martin Luther King.

Not a junior now, he still made a mark.
When M. L. played ball, he was the spark!
Basketballs, he touched, were shot in an arc;
This sure habit made kids call him, "Will Shoot!"

Reading of a man when he was near ten
Got him to consider time and again.
How he wished for the name of two great men -
This man and his dad, both stood for the truth.

A religious man who lived long ago
Said, "By the Bible, there's one thing I know
The teachings of the church cannot be so!"
Martin Luther suffered but held his stand.

M. L. asked his folks, "May I make a change?
I'll be Martin Luther, if you'll arrange."
M. L.'s parents thought it was good, not strange;
So, Michael took the Martin Luther name.

These would've been enough names for anyone,
But the new Martin Luther was not done.
Among his peers he was **the** special one -
A fine dancer and well liked by the girls.

See, Martin was known for his clothes so fine;
He was clean, neat and his shoes had a shine!
His wool tailored suits were smooth with each line
And earned him "Tweed" for another nickname.

Dr. King's nicknames seemed to never end;
Whether given by family or friend,
Although we can explain each nickname trend,
Dr. Martin Luther King is the name!

Up to Something

Three "peas in a pod" set out
To have fun every day.
They played pranks together in
Their *"up to something"* way!

Yes, they were *"peas in a pod"*.
Brothers and sis made three
Who played and shared together -
Chris, M. L. and A. D.

Yes, these *"peas in a pod"* were
Always **"up to something."**
They mostly did what was right
Or they'd face Daddy King.

With time to work, read and play
Arranged by Mother Dear,
There was no getting by her;
She made this very clear.

These three did not think it strange
They didn't try to get by
This daily routine. They didn't
Bother to ask her, "Why?"

How to use their money was
A lesson to be learned:
Save, share and spend equally
Money received or earned.

Taught their duty to mankind,
These three *"peas in a pod"*
Learned how to help other folks
And be true to their God.

Three "peas in a pod" set out
To have fun every day.
They played pranks together in
Their ***"up to something"*** way!

"A King Pledge for Peace"
(A tribute to the life and times of Dr. Martin Luther King, Jr.)

I promise to remember
      That peace begins with me.
I promise to remember
      All people should be free.
No matter what others do,
      I will stand for what is right
And fight all injustices
      With every bit of my might!

With all my power and strength,
      I promise to do my best
To give violence and hatred
      An eternal grave of rest!
I promise to remember
      The teachings of Dr. King.
I promise to remember
      The peace my love can bring.

SUGGESTED PROCEDURES: This poem has been used at the end of programs as a finale. Here are some ideas:

1. The audience may stand with right hand over their hearts while saying this pledge.
2. Having a well-rehearsed group leading this pledge is quite effective. One class or group may learn this pledge and serve as leaders.
3. The leading group should work on speaking clearly, distinctly, and as a chorus.
4. Putting the words on a screen or a printed program helps.

5. If this is your finale exercise, it is even better when a group or the audience sings, *"Let There be Peace on Earth"* after saying it.

Note: By the way, as a buyer of this book, you have permission to print this particular pledge on your printed program for your day of celebration.

Would I?

If I were a kid
With Martin Luther,
Would I say, "I did
All I could for others?"

Like the boy, Martin Luther,
Would defending another
Been something to occur
As part of my character?

When teasing by a bully
Caused kids to be in distress,
Would I have stood up truly
And tried to clear up the mess?

I am not sure, but I know
From now on I will indeed
Take steps to stop every foe
Of children who are in need.

When others needed a hand
With food, clothing or money.
Would I be one in this land
To help, not think it's funny?

When injustices stood up
And pushed other people down
Would I loathe that bitter cup
And help lift them from the ground?

Take a pledge along with me
To help others try to cope;
Take responsibility
To give broken kids some hope.

Then I'd say I would be like
Dr. Martin Luther King,
As I'd make a point to strike
Down every prejudiced thing!

Section 3:

Dramatizations

This section presents various dramas for individuals or small groups. As always, modify these works to suit your circumstances for the most effective presentation. Portions of this section are taken from larger works done by the author, Mrs. Elliott. The larger works will be available as individual products at a later date.

One Day. . .One Day!
A Monologue

Character: Martin Luther King, Jr. at the age of six wearing a cap and holding a napkin/handkerchief
Note: The names of the two White boys are not known, but Timmy and John are used here to provide clarity
Scene: Comfortable bedroom with pillows on bed, rocker, rug, mirror and a shelf with books, games, and a few toys
Time: August of 1935

(Storms into bedroom walking hard. Shows obvious angry. Stands on rug. Throws cap on the bed. Wipes away tears with the napkin/handkerchief.)

(Speaks as though in deep thought.) I don't get it. *(Stronger.)* I just don't get it! I never did anything to hurt them . . . not even their feelings. I just wanted them to come and play. I thought we'd go down the street to the firehouse. We hadn't gone there this week. We all love looking at the fire engine. Talking to the firemen is fun, too. John already said that he wants to be a firemen just like me.

(Sits on the bed. Hangs head a bit. Pauses. Lifts up head and speaks as if in deep thought.) I let them ride my bike. I even let Timmy use my **new** baseball glove and I used his old one! We have played together all this time . . . almost every day. What happened?

(Looks at hands turning them over and over.) I **LOOK** the same. *(Walks over to mirror. Looks at self carefully turning head side to side.)* I even **FEEL** the same.

(Touches face. Puts finger on cheek and thinks for a moment.) I just don't get it. I only asked if they could come out to play, *(Pauses.)* just like always. *(Slumps shoulders with head down.)*

(Sits in rocker and rocks for a moment. Wipes away a tear. Stops rocking and speaks softly.) Mama says that's the way things are because some **White** people don't understand that everybody is the same. *(Pauses.)* How can they not understand? When Timmy scraped his knees sliding into first base, he cried and bled just like I did when I fell down trying to catch that fly ball.   We both got **red** blood. *(Speaks a bit proudly.)* Well, I know I didn't cry as much as he did. He's such a crybaby! *(Pauses.)* But it still hurt!

(Stands. Goes to rug and turns toward rocker. Throws napkin/handkerchief in the rocker.   Hits fists in the air as though fighting someone. Stops.) Their mama was so mean! I only asked her why they couldn't come to play. She said, *(Speaks harshly and angrily imitating the boys' mother)* "Because they're White and you're a NEGRO!"

(Sits on the bed in disgust.) Well, I have been a Negro **all** my life. *(Pauses.)* So, what's wrong with **that**? *(Sarcastically.)* Besides, they are not really white. That lady must not understand anything! *(Pauses.)* John and Timmy love to come in **our** kitchen and get cookies and lemonade. *(Empathetically.)* Well, they won't get any more!

(Lets out a shriek or some type of small scream.) I am so MAD! *(Grabs a pillow and punches it a couple of times.)*   I am somebody. *(Tosses pillow aside and speaks a bit louder.)* I am somebody. *(Stands up tall and speaks even louder.)* I **am** somebody. Mother Dear told me so! *(Picks up cap and puts it on. Goes over to mirror and speaks even louder as if convincing the world.)* **I am somebody**.

(Returns to rocker and sits.) Why can't people understand that we are all the same? Why? *(Louder.)* Why? *(Boldly.)* I told Mother Dear that I'll change this when I grow up.

(Stands again. Looks in mirror. Stand as tall as possible. Speaks forcefully.) **I WILL!** *(Shakes forefinger at image of self in mirror.)* I'm going to turn this world upside down. *(Turns facing audience.)* Just wait! I don't know how, but I will find a way! One day . . . *(Raises fists in air and speaks confidently.)* **ONE DAY!**

"What Can I Do?"
(A Dialogue)

Characters: Martin and his friend, Billy, about age 10
Scene: Porch steps large enough for two boys on left side of stage with sidewalk slanting right toward audience; grass (lawn) on both sides of the sidewalk; other outdoor scenery; house seen in background.
Props: Plenty of grass blades for tossing
Time: Spring of 1937

(Martin sits on the steps of the walk leading to their home. He tosses grass or weeds occasionally as he whistles a tune. Billy walks over and stands beside him.)

Billy: Hey, M. L. What's happening?

Martin: Nothing much. I was just sitting here thinking.
Billy: *(Sits on steps beside him and joins in the tossing of the grass blades.)* About what?

Martin: Nothing really.

Billy: You sure?

Martin: Well. . .

Billy: *(Continues tossing grass blades.)* Well, what?

Martin: *(Sadly)* I heard my dad talking about Mr. Henry. He went to jail.

Billy: *(Stops tossing grass blades and looks at Martin.)* What happened?

Martin: He was stealing food for his family. It just doesn't seem right. *(Stops tossing grass blades and looks at Billy.)* I'm not saying it was right to steal. But, it just doesn't seem fair!

Billy: *(Both boys continue tossing grass blades. Speaks as if in deep thought.)* Seems like nothing is fair when it comes to us Black folks.

Martin: You got that right! I'll be glad when I can do something to change all this. But . . . *(Stops tossing grass blades and looks at Billy.)* what can I do?

Billy: Maybe not now, but when you grow up. And I can help, too. *(Shaking head affirmatively.)*

Martin: *(Annoyed, speaks strongly.)* When I grow up? It gets worse every day. *(Proudly.)* My daddy is always doing SOMETHING to show he doesn't like what he sees! *(Continues tossing grass blades.)* I hate these Jim Crow Laws.

Billy: I hate White people! *(Tosses grass blades forcefully.)*

Martin: *(Speaks quickly.)* Daddy said that we are to LOVE our enemies just like the Bible says.

Billy: *(A bit dejected.)* I know, but. . . They think they're better than us.

Martin: *(Looks confidently at Billy.)* Well, they AREN'T! *(Stops tossing grass blades and stands looking at Billy.)* Mother Dear said so! I am SOMEBODY! I like me! I LOVE-OVE-OVE me!

Billy: *(Stops tossing and stands facing Martin.)* Hey, Daddy King told us that in church last Sunday. *(Struts about a bit.)* He said to stand tall, trust God, and know you are somebody. *(Pushes out chest a bit to show pride. Sits down on lawn away from the steps.)*

Martin: *(Joins Billy on the grass. The boys continue to toss grass blades.)* That's what Daddy does all the time. He got them to change that elevator sign in City Hall downtown. Daddy wouldn't get off. *(Laughs.)* No White people could ride it for days! I guess they got tired of going up all those stairs. *(Both boys laugh.)*

Billy: Serves 'em right! What is Daddy King trying to change now?

Martin: I'm not sure, but he must be up to something. *(Both boys continue tossing grass blades.)* There's a whole lot of stuff Daddy can't stand here in Atlanta.

Billy: I know how he feels. *(Tosses grass blades angrily.)* I have to walk so far to school. Over two miles! I could go to that school a half mile away, but it's for the **White** kids. They even get to ride a bus to school.

Martin: They don't even have to walk a mile!

Billy: Yeah! It's not right! They have NEW books while my school gets their old, used up ones. *(Tosses a bunch of grass angrily.)*

Martin: I'm glad I go to my school. There is a lot of good stuff going on.

Billy: My reading book has **five** pages torn out! *(Tosses more grass blades.)* Sally let me copy the pages from her book. But that was a lot of work!

Martin: Mother Dear wants us to learn all we can. I just wish I could learn how to stop these Jim Crow Laws.

Billy: Me, too.

Martin: Did I tell you about that lady downtown?

Billy: What lady?

Martin: The one who slapped me! *(Tosses grass blades angrily.)*

Billy: She did what? *(Both boys stop tossing the blades.)*

Martin: *(Looks at Billy.)* Slapped me! And hard, too!

Billy: Why?

Martin: See, Mother Dear and I were downtown shopping. We had just left this store. *(Stands up and faces Billy.)* Out of nowhere, this White lady walked up to me and said, "You're that little Negro who stepped on my foot!" Before I could say anything, she slapped me! Right in front of Mother Dear!

Billy: *(Stands and faces Martin.)* Wow! What did y'all do?
Martin: We went on because we didn't want more trouble. I really learned what being slapped feels like! I found out what "Prejudice" means, too! *(Sits down.)*

Billy: *(Sits with Martin.)* What does it mean anyway?

Martin: It's when someone judges you or forms an opinion about you without the facts.

Billy: Oh. *(Speaks solemnly.)* Don't you just wish you could have hit her back?

Martin: Yeah, but Daddy said we should love our enemy. That's what the Bible says. It's best to obey the Bible and DADDY!

Billy: *(Looks down at feet.)* I know what you mean. *(Blows some grass blades in the air.)*

Martin: Daddy has a real way of standing up to White folks. *(Blows some grass blades in the air.)* I sometimes feel a little afraid because White people don't like "*uppity* " Negroes. *(Continues tossing blades.)* But Daddy says he will **never** accept things as they are. *(Thoughtfully.)* God has protected him all these years. I guess He will still protect him.

Billy: My Daddy never says much. *(Tosses blades angrily.)* He just goes on and takes stuff.

Martin: Last week, the police stopped us. Daddy was driving over to see Mr. Johnson. Daddy and I were laughing and talking. Daddy ran a stop sign because he was not paying attention.

Billy: Oh, no!

Martin: That White policeman was glad to stop us. He said, *(Imitating with a harsh, disrespectful voice.)* "Show me your license, BOY!"

Billy: White folks like to call all Black men "BOYS!" *(Tosses grass blades angrily.)*

Martin: *(Points forefinger to self.)* Well, Daddy pointed to me and said, "He's a **boy**. I'm a **man**. I won't talk to you until you call me one." *(Continues tossing grass blades.)*

Billy: *(Looks up at Martin.)* He said that?

Martin: Yeah! That policeman was so surprised! He could hardly write the ticket! *(Chuckles a bit.)*
Billy: *(Laughing.)* I wish I could have seen it.

Martin: My stomach was churning! I didn't know what he would do! Daddy told me later that all I have to do is look White folks straight in the eye. And they'll leave you alone.

Billy: *(Stops tossing grass blades and looks at Martin.)* Maybe **WE** should try that.

Martin: I think we better wait until we grow up.

Billy: *(Thoughtfully.)* Yeah, we better. *(Continues tossing.)*

Martin: I just wish I knew what to do.

Billy: Me, too.

Martin: *(Thinking for a moment.)* Hey! *(Stops tossing grass blades.)* I have an idea!

Billy: *(Looks at Martin and speaks eagerly.)* What?

Martin: We could run by Grant Park. *(Both boys stand.)* We can drink from the "White Only" fountain.

Billy: What if someone sees us?

Martin: Oh, we'll just look them **straight in the eye** and say, *(Mockingly.)* "Oh, I'm sorry, I didn't see any sign."

Billy: *(Both boys laugh heartedly.)* I can look innocent and I know YOU can!

Martin: *(Speaks confidently.)* Oh, yeah! Let's go! *(Both boys run off.)*

"I Remember"
(A Monologue)

Character: Miss Rebecca Dickerson who is about 75 years old, dressed matronly using a cane
Scene: Living room with rocker, end table with lamp and picture album, an old-fashion radio nearby
Sound: Ending of King's famous *"I Have a Dream"* speech, ovation and chorus of "We Shall Overcome"
Time: August 28, 1963

(Miss Dickerson stands by the radio listening to King's "I Have a Dream" speech. From the radio is heard from this point in the speech until its end: "And if America is to be a great nation…Thank God Almighty we are free at last." The ovation of the crowd is heard. Then a chorus of "We Shall Overcome." Miss Dickerson turns off the radio and goes to her chair walking a bit laboriously. She begins to speak as she sits down.)

Lord, Jesus. Have mercy. I remember that Martin. Smart as a whip! He was in my first grade class in August, hmmm, *(Thinking with finger on chin.)* let me see. . .about 1934 or was it 1935? I taught so many children it's hard to keep up with them. *(Forcefully.)* But there was none like that Martin! Now, of course I called him M. L. like everybody else. He came to Younge Street School as good as you please. Just beaming and glowing - eager to learn! Well, I just assumed he was six like all my other children.

I don't know why I didn't think about it, since I knew his mother, Alberta, real well. I had been a member at Ebenezer Baptist Church for as long as. . .I don't even remember when I wasn't a member! Her daddy, the Rev. Adam Daniel Williams, was a fine pastor.

Martin reminds me of him - trying to change things for the better. Once, Rev. Williams went to the publisher of *The Georgian* to talk as bold as you please. Well, that publisher was so shocked that a Black man came to see him, he invited him into his office. But when Rev. Williams asked that his newspaper stop being so insulting to Negroes that publisher yelled, "Get out of my office! Ain't no nigger gonna tell me how to run my paper!" But *(Shaking her finger.)* Rev. Williams fixed him good! He started a secret boycott and the Black folks didn't buy from any business that advertised in **that** newspaper. White folks couldn't understand what was happening. They lost so much money! One by one those businesses closed down! *(Laughing.)* Yeah. Every one of them! No more advertising from them for *The Georgian*. That high and mighty publisher got to eat a lot of **crow**! I only wish it had been Jim Crow that he was eating! So, *The Georgian* went bust just like the stock market during the Great Depression.

Now, Daddy King didn't show any slack either. He made them remove that sign in City Hall! Whites and Blacks could not ride the elevator at the same time back then. So Daddy King got on the elevator and rode it all day long! Day after day! Those white folks got so tired of walking up and down all those stairs that somebody took down the sign! Then, Daddy King rode on the elevator **with** the White folks. I'm glad he kept going to the Atlanta School Board! Finally, they gave the **same** pay for us Black teachers that the Whites teachers received. Besides, we had to work harder with more children, less materials **and** in rundown school buildings. I dare think that's why I am in poor health now. Lord, I worked so hard for so long in those drafty buildings! *(Proudly.)* But how our children learned!

Now here is Martin today taking up the fight in Washington, D. C.! He was a great kid. It broke my heart to send him home. The school rule was that children had to be six years old, no matter how smart they were. It was a Wednesday. The boys were drawing that day and just talking quietly like kids do. Jimmy was so proud of his birthday party on the past Saturday that he started telling about his cake and all.   There was little Martin trying to fit in so he started talking about **his** birthday cake.

When he told about those **five** candles and not six, I started thinking. He was a year and a half younger than Chris. She had come to first grade that year, too. They weren't twins. . .I knew that! I had no choice. I had to send him home. Oh, how he stood silently with tears streaming down his little face. He wanted to learn so much. He was already an outstanding reader far beyond the other children.

Yeah, Alberta apologized. She said that M. L. had begged so hard, she finally gave in and let him go to school. I know she wished she had enrolled him in that university school, but they were all filled up by then. Of course, Alberta was a teacher herself. She just kept right on teaching M. L. at home.

When he returned the next year, that child was so far ahead of the other kids, I just had to send him on to second grade. *(Sigh.)* I lost him again. Just seeing him around the school growing and learning was a real pleasure. I admit I would have had much more pleasure with him in **MY** class.

In a year or so, I got A. D. in my class. Now, he was different as all sisters and brothers are. He was a fair student, but he was more concerned about playing than learning. Yes, A. D. was a challenge. *(Laughing softly.)* When Daddy King came to school to see about him, that did it! He worked hard to behave from then on. I know he didn't want another lesson from Daddy King. My lessons were a whole lot nicer. He was just all boy. He loved to tease! *(Giggling.)* Once, M. L. even hit him on the head with the telephone because he wouldn't stop teasing Chris! He wasn't a mean child, just mischievous.

Now M. L. was mischievous, too, but he knew how to talk his way out of trouble. M. L. wasn't a teaser. Most time when he got in trouble, he was trying to help someone else. How he hated bullies. With his little self, he was always standing up to some bigger child defending another child. He got into more scraps that way. He was **strong** for his size. I guess he got tired of being hit; so, he started challenging the bullies to "go to the grass" which meant whoever got the other down first won. *(Laughing.)* It was just like M. L. to come up with a new idea to give **him** the advantage.

I tell you when he decided to out talk the other kids, *(Laughing.)* they didn't stand a chance. *(Leans back in rocker and starts rocking.)* He seemed to relish the idea that he could use words to get others to do what **he** wanted. Most times though, the kids didn't know what the words meant that he said. They just gave up. No way could they out talk him! *(Laughing.)* Lord, what a child! He seemed driven to learn more and more words. When the school had any contest or recitations, M. L. was the star.

There was Chris, the oldest of the three, but she couldn't compete with M. L. She was a sweet child. Now, she got into devilment, too. Lord, have mercy! How those three King kids would scare folks near to death. My friend, Priscilla, was passing by the Kings there on Auburn Street one evening just before dark. I think she was with her sister, Martha. They were just talking and enjoying the walk home. When they saw that animal, they screamed! Being city ladies, they did not take to the idea of seeing some wild animal on the sidewalk. The whole neighborhood heard those two! The man across the street came running to the rescue. *(Tossing hand forward.)*

Humph! It was just those kids - up to some prank. There they were hiding in the hedges by the sidewalk, mind you. With Grandma Jeannie's fine fox fur piece tied on the end of a stick, they shook it making the ladies think it was real.

I believe *(Shakes forefinger a couple of times.)* they got in a lot of trouble with Daddy King that time. Alberta was soft and gentle, but they couldn't pull the wool over her eyes. She was firm when it mattered. But Daddy King was quick on the draw! Not so much with Chris, though. Of course, Grandma Jeannie would always take up for M. L. I know he was her favorite. I don't care how much she denied it! She loved them all, but M. L. was real special to her. *(Sadly, shaking head from side to side.)* M. L. really took it hard when Grandma Jeannie died. He was sad for the longest time.

Yes, I remember. Oh, I remember so much! During the Depression, so many people depended on the Kings and the Ebenezer Baptist Church. How the Kings bagged up their own groceries! They even got medicine for my mother when she was so sick and I was waiting for my first paycheck. If they hadn't got the medicine then, no telling what would have happened to her. That pneumonia can be tricky, especially when people get older. The dinners I ate at their house. Hmmmmm good!

(Gets up. Puts on hat and gloves.) I reckon I better get up and get down to the church. Don't want to miss prayer meeting tonight. Probably be lots of talk about Martin and that March on Washington, today. Martin made me mighty proud today! Lord, help Martin! Help **us** Black folks! It is time. I won't forget the past. I will remember the struggles. *(Raises hands and looks upward.)* I will praise you, Lord, for each victory! *(Goes out.)*

"Lord, that Child"
(A Monologue)

Character: Alberta King, a concerned mother dressed modestly wearing an apron with a crumble note in the pocket.
Scene: Comfortable, well-decorated bedroom with rocker and small table beside where a Bible lays
Sound: Soft singing by a choir of a Negro Spiritual
Time: About 1938 in November

(Soft music is heard. Mrs. King enters the bedroom. She seems troubled. She sits in rocker and picks up the Bible. She opens the Bible, but puts on it her lap in a moment without reading it. Music fades. She looks upward and begins to speak.)

Now, Lord, You have been so good to my family and me all these years. As long as I can remember, You have provided all we needed. Thank You, Lord that we have been blessed to share with many. It is a joy to share Your goodness with others. I thank You for that privilege.

(Closes the Bible and lays it aside.) I especially thank You for the blessings of my three children, Chris, A. D., and M. L. But Lord I really need Your help. I just don't know what to do about Martin. But, Lord, You know! He's a good child, but so different. How do I raise him to be the man YOU want him to be? I try to teach him to do right. *(Takes Bible and holds it up.)* I even have him learn Your word. But it seems there is always something else that I don't know how to handle. Now Daddy will use that belt on him in a minute. Is that the right thing? That child will just stand and take all you give him without a sound. I know it hurts. I can hardly stand to be in the same room. M. L. just stands there saying nothing with a few tears streaming down his little face. He doesn't look angry, just hurt.

Are we doing more damage than good? Your word says that if I spare the rod, I'll spoil the child. But what kind of rod should we use with M. L.?

Just like the other week, Lord. He was standing there looking so dejected after hitting A. D. on the head with the phone. Now, he knew better. But there he was in trouble again trying to help somebody else. He couldn't get A. D. to leave Chris alone so he took matters in his own hands. He LAID A. D. out! Lord, *(Shaking head from side to side.)* what do I do with this child? He had to be punished. He can't do wrong to make something right. I felt so sorry for him.

Now, my Momma. . .that's another story! She just thinks we shouldn't ever spank him. *(Mockingly.)* "He's such a GOOD little boy," she always says. Well. . .*(Pauses.)* he is, but he has to learn not to hurt others. *(Walks around room. Thinks a moment. Looks up.)* Doesn't he? *(Sits in rocker. Puts head in both hands and moves head side to side. Looks up as if mourning. Speaks softly.)* Lord. . . *(A bit louder shaking head from side to side.) Lord, that Child!* Tell me what to do! He's so young and sensitive. Lord, You know he's very strong-willed and determined to make **his** point? I want him to grow up wanting to **help** others, not to **hurt** them.

How do I get his Daddy to just listen to M. L.'s side of the story this time? He already has a bruised eye from standing up to James this time. What a bully that boy is! He took Sally's lunch and ate her cookie. It seems this boy is always bothering her. Probably because she cries so easily.   M. L. just had to take matters into his hands again!

(Takes crumbled note from apron pocket. Looks at it. Holds it up for a moment as she speaks.) Now, I have to give Daddy this note from the teacher. M. L. was in a fight again! Lord,

he's so small anyway. The bullies can usually outdo him. What a spirited little boy!   He just won't back down. The same way he acts when he gets punished. Lord, I know he has to be disciplined, but give his Daddy a soft heart this time. Please-e-e-e-e-e! God, please help us with this child! I really need Your help! No one else can help me, now. *(Looks about room.)* Well, it's about time for Daddy to come home. I better finish dinner. *(Looks up.)* Lord, just don't forget. I'm counting on YOU.

Living with the Kings*

Features only two Acts of the actual play which can be done Independently

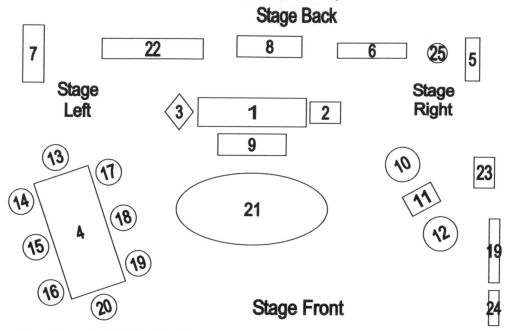

1 – Comfortable Sofa
2 – End Table with Phone
3 – Floor Lamp or on a Table
4 – Dinner Table with Flowers
5 – Front Door
6 – Book Shelf
7 – Kitchen Entrance
8 – Door to Bathroom
9 – Coffee Table with Books
10 – Arm Chair
11 – End Table with Lamp
12 – Arm Chair
13 – Daddy King's Chair
14 – Mother Dear's Chair
15 – Guest Chair
16 – Guest Chair
17 – A. D.'s Chair
18 – Christine's Chair
19 – M. L.'s Chair
20 – Grandma Jeannie's Chair
21 – Area Rug
22 – Chest/Credenza with Centerpiece
23 – Chime Clock
24 – Entrance to Upstairs
25 – Hat Rack
26 – Window

Two or three pictures may be added. Room should be inviting, comfortable, and well-coordinated.

Setting

The home of the Kings at 501 Auburn Street in Atlanta, GA in the late 1930's

Characters

Christine – About age 9
M. L. – Age 8, smallest boy
A. D. – Age 7, but slightly larger than M. L.   —— Act 1
Mother Dear
Tim – Age 8 largest boy

Christine – About age 9
M. L. – About age 8, smallest boy
A. D. – Nearly age 7, but slightly larger than M. L.   —— Act 2
Mother Dear
Daddy King
Mr. Brown – Neighbor

Sound Effects- Act 1

Opera Music   Chime Clock - 4:30   Rustling leaves
Doorbell

Sound Effects- Act 2

Doorbell   Music

Other Items Needed

Act 1	Act 2
Numerous books	Same as Act 1, except
Homework sheet for A. D.	Newspaper
Pencils	Cap for Mr. Brown
Crayons	Small box with coins
Tablet for Chris	Handkerchief or cloth
Apron for Mother Dear	Slippers for Daddy King
Football for Tim	Pocket spinning top for A. D.

ACT I

Featuring: **M. L.**   **A. D.**   **Chris**   **Mother Dear**   **Tim**

(Opera plays softly in the background. Curtains open with the three King children quietly reading or writing. Chime clock strikes four thirty. Opera music fades. Christine is writing and drawing while sitting in the front armchair (12) on Stage Right. M. L. is sitting on the floor in front of the sofa Stage Left of the Coffee Table (9). A. D. is sitting on the sofa by the phone (2). All is quiet for a moment.)

A. D.: *(Walks over behind Chris and peers over her shoulder.)* What're you drawing, Chris?

Chris: *(Annoyed, she looks up at A. D.)* None of your business! *(Closes tablet and holds up to chest.)* I am drawing something for Mama. It's a secret.

A. D.: *(Stands on the side of Chris but faces audience, folds hands under chin as if praying and begging.)* Oh, come on. Please-e-e-?

Chris: No. Go draw your own picture.

A. D.: *(Steps forward and reaches for the tablet. Chris moves tablet away from him.)* Let me see. I'll show you what's in my pocket. *(Puts hand on pocket as if to hide item.)*

Chris: *(Holds tablet on the side of chair toward audience.)* I said "NO!" I don't care what's in your pocket. *(Loudly.)* I'll call Mother Dear if you don't stop.

A. D.: *(Reaches for tablet again.)* I just want to see it. *(Stomps his foot.)*

Mother Dear: *(Calls from the kitchen (7).)* What is going on out there? You know it's time to read and study. It should be quiet now.

Chris: *(She sits on her tablet. Turns her back to A. D. Turns her head towards audience.   Starts reading her book.)* Leave me alone. You're supposed to be reading or studying.

A. D.: *(Looking dejected, sits on sofa roughly.)* I read already. Besides, I don't have anything to study.

M. L.: *(Looks up from his book and speaks to A. D.)* I thought you said you had to learn your multiplication tables. I'll help you.

A. D.: *(Slumps down and holds his book up to cover his face.)* I don't want your help. I can do it myself.

M. L.: *(Returns to reading.)* OK, but I will be glad to drill you with the cards. Let me know if you change your mind.

(All is quiet for a moment. Rustling leaves are heard outside.)

A. D.: *(Rushes to the window (26) and looks out. Speaks excitedly.)* It's Tim. I bet he wants to play! He's got his football.

Chris: *(Raises up in chair to look out the window (26).)* You can't go out to play anyway! This is not playtime. *(She sits down and returns to reading her book.)*

(Martin gets up and starts for the front door just before the doorbell rings.)

A. D.: *(Rushes to door.)* I want to get it. Let me. *(Martin opens door.)* Shucks!

M. L.: Hi, Tim. See you got your football.
Tim: *(Steps inside as Martin and A. D. step back.)* Yeah. Can you come out to play? It's still daylight.

A. D.: *(Eagerly shaking head up and down.)* I want to play.

M. L.: *(Looks at A. D.)* You know we can't. *(Looks at Tim.)* It's our study time, Tim.

Tim: *(Speaks braggingly.)* I'm glad I don't have to study. I did my chores. My ma says I can play till it gets dark.

A. D.: *(Holds head down slightly.)* I wish I didn't have to read or study.

M. L.: *(Speaking confidently.)* I love to read and study.

Tim: Not me!

A. D.: Me neither. *(Goes near door of kitchen (7) and calls to Mother Dear.)* Mother Dear, may I please go out to play now?

Mother Dear: *(Comes to the door and looks at A. D.)* You know you can't. Your Dad will be home soon and it will be dinnertime. Bring me your work. Let me see what you have been doing.

(A. D. goes to sofa to get his book and paper. Mother Dear notices Tim.)

Mother Dear: Oh, hi, Tim. The children are doing their work, now.

Tim: *(Waves.)* Hi, Mrs. King. I guess I better go home. *(Speaks to the kids.)* See yah, later. Bye.

Three King Kids: *(In unison)* Bye.

(Tim closes door. A. D. takes his paper and book to Mother Dear.)

Mother Dear: *(Wipes hands on her apron and takes paper and book from A. D. She looks over the paper carefully and then at A. D.)* You did most of this right, but you have three mistakes to correct. You need to work more carefully. Think, A. D. You have a **good** head on your shoulders. *(Rubs his head and gives him a hug.)* Find your mistakes and change your answers before dinner. *(Hands paper and book to A. D. and returns to the kitchen (7).)*

A. D.: *(Shrugs his shoulders and drags slowly to the sofa. Picks up his pencil and begins looking over the paper. Mumbles to himself.)* I did work carefully.

Chris: *(Walking over to A. D.)* Do you want me to help you?

M. L.: Mother Dear told **him** to do it.

Chris: *(Puts hand on her hips and looks at Martin.)* I know that! *(Looks at A. D.)* If you need help, I'll ask Mother Dear if I can help, OK?

A. D.: *(Sulk, but turns face away from kitchen door.)* OK. *(Room darkens as Opera music begins to fades in softly. Curtains close.)*

Act 2

Featuring: **Daddy King** **Mr. Brown** **Mother Dear** **M. L.** **Chris** **A. D.**

(Lights slowly brighten showing the family all in the living room. A. D. is showing his paper to Mother Dear as they sit on the sofa. M. L. is reading a book while lying on his stomach on the rug. Chris is drawing in her tablet sitting at the dining table in chair (16). Daddy King is reading the newspaper sitting in armchair (12). Suddenly doorbell rings urgently.)

Daddy King*: (Still reading the newspaper.)* Boys, get the door.

(M. L. and A. D. go to the door and open it.)

Mr. Brown: *(Nervously urgent.)* Is Daddy King home?

M. L. and A. D.: *(In unison.)* Yes, sir.

(Chris and Mother Dear lookup at Mr. Brown.)

Daddy King: *(Lays paper on end table (11) and leans forward to see Mr. Brown.)* Excuse me *(Not getting up)* but my feet are "dog" tired tonight. Come on in. *(Waves hand inviting him in.)* Have a seat.

(M. L. and A. D. step back to let Mr. Brown in. They return to their work. Chris continues to draw.)

Mr. Brown: *(Removes cap as he comes in and folds it in his hand. Stands beside Daddy King.)* I don't mean to bother you, but we need help. I don't know where to go. I went to my family and even tried to work downtown, but I can't find any work. *(Sticks cap in back pocket.)* You know the lumber company

closed down last month. Wife and the kids are feeling real poor.
I'm out of money. The electric company is gonna turn off my
lights, 'less I pay $6.13 tomorrow! *(Begins wringing his hands.)*
Can you help me? *(Moves head repeatedly left to right.)* I don't
know what we gonna do!

Daddy King: Now, you know we will do SOMETHING.
(Motioning hand towards armchair (10).) Just sit down and we'll
see what we can do. Do you have enough food for the week?

Mr. Brown: *(Sits down politely and speaks more calmly.)* Yes,
Daddy King.   Thanks to your church, Ebenezer. I went by there
yesterday and they filled our basket with food. We thank God for
what you do for all of us.

Daddy King: *(Speaking to Mother Dear.)* How much we have
left in the fund, Bunch?

Mother Dear: *(Looks up at the men.)* Well, Mrs. Adams needed
$3 for medicine on Monday. I'm not sure, but there must be a
few dollars. I hope it is enough.

(M. L. goes over to Mother Dear and whispers in her ear.)

Daddy King: *(Firmly with a hint of disappointment in his voice.)*
Now Martin, you know it is not polite to whisper in front of our
guest.

M. L.: *(Hangs head a bit.)* I'm sorry, Daddy. *(Looks at Daddy
King.)* Excuse me, Daddy, but I was just telling Mother Dear that
there is some money left from the singing program I did two
Sundays ago. *(Excitedly with head up now.)* The church raised
more than $12!

Daddy King: That's more than is needed.

Mr. Brown: Bless you, dear child.

Daddy King: *(Speaks in a matter-of-fact tone.)* Oh, it's all right Mr. Brown. M. L. knows we must share with others. It is our duty as children of God. We are always happy to help.

(Mother Dear and M. L. leave the room going out entrance (24). A. D. tags along.)

Daddy King: Well, tell me, are they going to re-open the lumberyard soon?

Mr. Brown: *(Sounding hopelessly.)* At first I thought they would, but this Depression is real bad. Nobody is hiring either. Not even to work in the fields.

Daddy King: Some of the farmers I know couldn't even buy seeds to plant. Their harvest is really small this year. They don't even have anything to take to the market.

Mr. Brown: Wife did do some washing and ironing for Miss Evans last week, but *that $3 is gone. Couldn't find nobody to work for this week. She been feeling poorly anyway.*

(Mother Dear and the boys return through entrance (24). M. L. hands a small box of coins to Daddy king who counts out $6.13 and puts the rest in the box which he places on the table (11).)

Mother Dear: It is a lot of coins, King; put them in this. *(She hands him the handkerchief.)*

(Daddy King ties coins in the handkerchief and hands it to Mr. Brown.)

Mr. Brown: *(Grins and stands.)* Oh, that's just fine; they spent, too. Well, I hate to leave, but I want to let the wife know we can pay tomorrow. That may make her feel a whole lot better.

(Chris and Daddy King stand up.)

Daddy King: *(Shaking Mr. Brown's hand.)* We certainly understand. Just take care of yourselves. *(Walks him to the door as other family members look on)* See you Sunday at church. Bye.

Mr. Brown: *(Backing out the door.)* Bye, everybody. *(Bows slightly.)* God bless you Daddy King.

Mother Dear: Bye. I hope your wife and children feel better soon.

Chris: Bye.

A. D.: Bye.

M. L.: Bye.

(Daddy King shakes his head repeatedly from side to side as he returns to reading his newspaper. Others return to original position for this Act.)

Daddy King: *(Sadly.)* I'm glad we could help, but Lord knows it's getting mighty tight around here. So many people need help.

Mother Dear: *(Sadly.)* Sure do. Mrs. Nelson needed some sugar and flour again. I know she hates to ask. I told her if she needed it, she was welcomed to it.

Daddy King: *(Looks around the room at them.)* Children, remember when God blesses you, you must share. That's why we teach you how to Save, Share, and Spend your money.

Mother Dear: It is the best way to learn how to help others and yourself. *(Looking around at the children.)* Don't ever forget no matter where you go or how much you have. Share one-third with the Church and others, save one-third, and then, you can spend the other third on yourself. Do you children understand?

All Kids: *(Shaking their heads affirmatively, speaking in unison.)* Yes, ma'am.

Mother Dear: Well, it's bedtime. We ALL have a long day tomorrow. Go on up and get ready for bed. We will come up and have prayer with you, later.

(Children exit through entrance (24).)

Daddy King: Lord, I thank You that You gave us everything we needed for this day!

Mother Dear: And He will take care of tomorrow, too. Praise the Lord! *(Sits in armchair (10). The Kings reach out and take each other's hand. They look lovingly in each other's eyes.)*

(As they share a moment of happiness, the room slowly darkens while music slowly increases in volume.)

REFERENCES

Adler, David A. A Picture Book of Martin Luther King, Jr. New York, United States: Holiday House, 1989.

Boone - Jones, Margaret. MLK, Jr.: a Picture Story. Chicago, United States: Children's Press, 1968.

DeKay, James T. Meet MLK, Jr. New York, United States: Random House, 1969.

Farris, Christine King. My Brother Martin. New York, United States: Simon & Schuster Books for Young Readers, 2003.

Hilgartner Schlank, Carol and Barbara Metzger. Martin Luther King, Jr.: a Biography for Young Children. Mt Rainier, United States Of America: Gryphon House, 1990.

Mattern, Joanne. Young Martin Luther King, Jr.: "I Have a Dream". Troll Associates, 2001.

Millender, Dharathula H. Martin Luther King, Jr.: Boy with a Dream. Indianapolis, United States: The Bobbs (Hilgartner Schlank and Metzger) - Merrill Co., Inc, 1969.
1971.

Young, Margaret B. The Picture Life of Martin Luther King, Jr. New York, United States: Franklin Watts, 1968

3384742